On *Title and*

"A haunting and often fiercely funny meditation on life as a state of permanent exile...The marvel of Mr. Eno's voice is how naturally it combines a carefully sculptured lyricism with sly, poker-faced humor. Everyday phrases and familiar platitudes—'Don't ever change,' 'Who knows'—are turned inside out or twisted into blunt, unexpected punch lines punctuating long rhapsodic passages that leave you happily word-drunk."

—Charles Isherwood, *New York Times*

"The piece proves to be an always fascinating and surprisingly moving seventy minutes of theatre...What emerges from his humorous, sometimes stream-of-conscious patter is a heartfelt exploration of the transience of everything in this life, from words themselves, to relationships, to our very existence."

—Andy Propst, *TheaterMania*

"*Title and Deed* is daring within its masquerade of the mundane, spectacular within its minimalism and hilarious within its display of po-faced bewilderment. It is a clown play that capers at the edge of the abyss...Eno's voice is unique; his play is stage poetry of a high order. You can't see the ideas coming in *Title and Deed.* When they arrive–tiptoeing in with a quiet yet startling energy—you don't quite know how they got there. In this tale's brilliant telling, it is not the narrator who proves unreliable but life itself. The unspoken message of Eno's smart, bleak musings seems to be: enjoy the nothingness while you can."

—John Lahr, *New Yorker*

"Pensive, lyrical, deeply funny and profoundly sad."

—Marilyn Stasio, *Variety*

On *Oh, the Humanity and other good intentions*

"If you've ever had an urge to drop to your knees begging 'can somebody help me please?' or wanted to admit 'I don't know, I just don't know,' then these five playlets by Will Eno are for you…Eno is a supreme monologist, using a distinctive, edgy blend of non sequiturs and provisional statements to explore the fragility of our existence, the way we determinedly cling on even when 'the rug is disintegrating thread by thread, gone before it can be pulled from underneath us.' There are a lot of words, but they are always exquisitely chosen… *Oh, the Humanity* reveals that we are beautiful walking tragedies blinking with absurd optimism into the camera lens of history."

—Lyn Gardner, *Guardian*

"Funny and tragic and truthful…for the uninitiated, *Oh, the Humanity* provides a perfect introduction to Eno's work… Made up of five short plays, this is stripped back drama that is all about rich dialogue and big ideas."

—*What'sOnStage*

"Mr. Eno's unmistakable voice—aggressively stylized, unendingly compassionate, flecked with weird, bleak humor—rings out with the same arresting originality in this hour-long evening of playfully profound theater…Mr. Eno dares to believe that the theatre is the natural forum for a collective reckoning with the brutal truths and the consoling beauties of experience—all those big-ticket items that you blush to discuss publicly. His despairing figures lay bare their lonely, wounded hearts without blinking, holding mirrors up to our own. What better place for such an encounter? At the theatre, after all, we can feel most powerfully a sense of communion in life's solitude. It is a place to go to feel alone together."

—Charles Isherwood, *New York Times*

TITLE AND DEED

OH, THE HUMANITY

BOOKS BY WILL ENO
AVAILABLE FROM TCG

The Flu Season and Other Plays

ALSO INCLUDES:

Intermission
Tragedy: a tragedy

Gnit

Middletown

The Realistic Joneses [forthcoming]

Thom Pain (based on nothing)

Title and Deed/
Oh, the Humanity and Other Good Intentions

TITLE AND DEED

monologue for a slightly foreign man

OH, THE HUMANITY

and other good intentions

Will Eno

THEATRE COMMUNICATIONS GROUP
NEW YORK
2014

Title and Deed/ Oh, the Humanity and other good intentions is published by Theatre Communications Group, Inc., 520 Eighth Avenue, 24th Floor, New York, NY 10018-4156

"Behold the Coach, in a Blazer, Uninsured" appeared in a slightly different version in *Harper's Magazine*, February 2003.

This volume is published in arrangement with Oberon Books Ltd, 521 Caledonian Road, London, N7 9RH.

This publication is made possible in part by the New York State Council on the Arts with the support of Governor Andrew Cuomo and the New York State Legislature.

TCG books are exclusively distributed to the book trade by Consortium Book Sales and Distribution.

A catalogue record for this book is available from the Library of Congress.

ISBN 978-1-55936-465-2 (paperback)

ISBN 978-1-55936-777-6 (ebook)

Front cover image by Simon Larbalestier, "Desert Storm 2001"

Back cover image by Rodolfo Clix/Stock.ZCHNG

First Edition, September 2014

Contents

TITLE AND DEED

To Jim Houghton, now and forever

Title and Deed was first performed at The Alice Griffin Jewel Box Theatre on May 8 2012 with the following cast:

Man: **Conor Lovett**

Creative Team

Director: **Judy Hegarty Lovett**

Set Designer: **Christine Jones**

Costume Designer: **Andrea Lauer**

Lighting Designer: **Ben Stanton**

Production Stage Manager: **Donald Fried**

United States Premiere originally produced by Signature Theatre (James Houghton, Founding Artistic Director; Erika Mallin, Executive Director) in association with Gare St Lazare Players Ireland in the Alice Griffin Jewel Box Theatre at The Pershing Square Signature Center. Opening: May 20, 2012.

Signature Theatre is a not-for-profit organization founded in 1991 by James Houghton. The company exists to honor and celebrate the playwright. Signature makes an extended commitment to a playwright's body of work, and during this journey the writer is engaged in every aspect of the creative process. Signature is the first theatre company to devote an entire season to the work of a single playwright, including re-examinations of past writings as well as New York and world premieres. By championing in-depth explorations of a living playwright's body of work, Signature delivers an intimate and immersive journey into the playwright's singular vision.

Dramatis Personae

MAN

Setting

the theater, a room, the present

Characters

just a man; ideally, he is slightly foreign to his audience, though a native speaker of English

Wardrobe

simple, normal

Props

a bag or backpack containing a three-foot-long section of a wooden broomstick and a metal lunch box.

Lights up on MAN, *just arriving in the middle of the stage, carrying a bag, which he sets down, at some point in the opening few lines.*

MAN: I'm not from here. I guess I never will be. That's how being from somewhere works. I'll assume you are, though. That'll make everything make a little more, I think your word is, sense. And it might help to move things along. Let's hope. We don't need to hope. Things move quickly enough. In fact, we're practically almost done. It's my word, too, by the way, "sense." Oh, so, one other thing – don't hate me, if you wouldn't mind. Thanks. I know that's not something you can ask a person. But, you know, what is? So, yeah, don't walk out on me, or, if you do, try to walk out quietly. Keep the screaming to yourself, if you could, as we used to say back in the sand pits. Thanks. *(Small gesture towards bag.)* That's just a bag, by the way. Just some unattended luggage. No, seriously, don't worry, it's just my bag, a couple of belongings.

People don't gather enough, anymore. Where I'm from, we used to gather all the time – Midwinter's Eve, or for Reverse Weddings, or for something we had called Terrible Saturdays. So, yeah, thank you, and, welcome – it's nice to see a little clump.

Anyway, let's get back down to earth, to my arrival here, and I mean, just, here. The aeroporto, I think none of us calls it. Customs. I was one of the first people in the wrong line, and then someone helped me out, and I was suddenly the last person in the right one. And then, you've done this, through the zigzags, kicking the suitcase, and finally up to the welcome sign and bulletproof glass. I remember my mouth suddenly getting dry and my eyes starting to water, like I was about to lie, even though I wasn't. Maybe other people know that feeling? The truth in the heart, the lump in the throat. "Business or pleasure?," the man asked. "Neither," says I, jauntily. "I'm here to save us all." "And who is us?," he asked, writing. "Exactly," I said, with a wink, though I would never wink and jauntily's not the right word. The man looked at me. "Seriously," he said. "Just visiting," I said. "All right," he said. I believe I have that verbatim. A number lit up over his head, a nice six in your local governmental font. "Business or pleasure," he said, to the next one of me, some other version who'd just blown in, full of hope and in the wrong clothes for the climate, and I was on to the next line. They scanned a photo of my retina. "Can I get a copy of that," I said, "for a, you know, for a keepsake?" They said, in the local parlance, "No." Then I was in. Then I was here. I don't know why international travel puts me in such a puckish mood. Maybe it's the free coffee or the lack of sleep and oxygen. Maybe it's a little hopeless glimmer of hope that I might somehow, with a change of scenery, change. Or the new bacteria, or, just, it's exciting.

Keepsake is a word we won't look into any further, though I bet the right type of person on the right lonely night could give himself a pretty good cry by doing the etymology. Or, herself. Trace the origin of any word and, if you're half a man, and I can say without bragging I am, or half a woman, which is sort of my type, you'll shed some serious tears at the long and trembling history of these frail little sounds, made up out of nowhere. Lamp.

Horse. Shed. It's like loss and wandering and some strange German joy are built right in, somehow. They almost make you want to cry, or make you want to do something else, almost. Words. Ah, but they do the job. If you need a lamp or a horse. If you live in a shed and you're lost and trying to get home.

What next? Let me see. Let me stand here for a second and see.

The next part of my great voyage we can probably skip. It would just be different scenes of me in other lines, reading schedules, trying to get change, wishing I were home. Home where I'm from, that is, home where the hat's hanging and the placenta's buried. I doubt you've ever heard of it. Or, maybe some of you… *(Very brief pause, and he somewhat defensively moves on.)* No, I doubt you have, and, of course, that's fine. It's just a little thing, my country – down by the sea, roughly, or near the mountains, seasonal enough, a small population, the chief exports sarcasm and uric acid. No, but I'm proud of her, the old girl. The very old woman. The lying-dying senile old mess, so far away, her milky eyes trying to focus on anything and her mouth opening and closing for some reason other than to speak.

Maybe that's strange of me, to make a thing into a person, and then to make the person a weak and dying one. I don't know if I do it out of love or one of the other feelings. Maybe you're doing something similar, right now. Making something into something else and then somehow killing the second thing. Who knows. I'm looking into your eyes and saying: Who knows. It's scary but kind of interesting to think the answer is: nobody. *(Brief pause.)*

The eyes are the window of the eyes. I'm trying to remember who said that. *(Very brief pause.)* It was a guy I used to paint houses with. Brian.

Oh. Time to share. *(He gets the three-foot piece of broomstick out of the bag.)* This is a nice one of these, yeah? Maybe I'll play a little something for you, later. I'm kidding – it's not an instrument, it's just a stick, just one of my belongings. A belonging of mine. I could probably get a sound out of it, though.

(Puts the stick back in the bag, or on top of it, at some point in the next couple of lines.) I remember, back when I wasn't here, there was always this thunder, this kind of, not really, thunder, there. I don't know what that was. Just always in the background, rolling, kind of threatening, or soothing. For a long time I

thought it was inside my head. I could have asked. I don't know what they could've told me. But, anyway, thunder. A kind of steady beating, and a lot of rain, or a lot of gray skies, or a lot of blue skies under which we worried about rain. Anyway, the sky made so much noise I could never sleep, even as a child, even before that, even if it was in my head. I remember learning to read, late one rumbling night. My father came through the room to get a glass of water. "Don't move your lips," he said. "You're moving your lips." And that sound outside the house went on, or got a little louder. I know you have all that here, normal weather patterns and fathers walking through rooms and sound waves and so on. But it's different. The rain's not as rainy, or something, and the howl of my ancestors, or whatever that is, it sounds more like an ear infection, here, or some neurological thing.

Maybe this is progress, maybe that's what the world sounds like. Or maybe I'm romanticizing.

I don't want to paint too dreary a picture of the misery. Because I've laughed, in my life. In fact, on one particular full moon, I remember, I laughed until the sun came up, until things suddenly didn't seem that funny anymore. And I've been to the dances, the dances that anyone could go to, and I have supped at the…at the what? The table of something. I don't know how to finish that. *(A very small, quick, flourish.)* Olé.

Don't pity me, is all I'm saying, plus this, which is that I have loved, romantically. And, just as unbelievably, I've been loved.

And there can be no finer state. It's a many-splintered thing. Is that Shakespeare? Or, I just remembered, it was that same guy Brian. My thing is, I speak to you as a foreigner, yes, but also as a lucky person, as a recipient of one of the blessings our little planetarium can bestow. I assure you I'm here as a celebrant, tone and vocabulary aside. I have a sad way of talking, but that's just my voice. It's just the sound of my voice.

(Very brief pause.) We all have happy memories. We all have a funny little map in our head that divides the world into home and away.

There's a tradition, where I'm from, something started by the elders, a beautiful institution, maybe you have it here, where, having settled on your intended, you sit outside the window, or the door, or at the end of the street, and you wait, and you do not move. Maybe you flinch from time to time, or you wince here and there, because why wouldn't you wince, but mainly you stay still and wait. You sit and daydream and make plans in your head, plans for your future happiness. Then the time comes for you to move. Here, the tradition insists you go and get the saddest instrument you don't know how to play. Most people reach for the cello, given the difficulty and mournfulness of it, but I chose instead, when it was my time, a tuba. I weighed less, when I was courting Lauren, and needed the extra heft. No, I probably weighed the same, but I may have felt less – God, what did I feel less of? – less landlocked? I doubt that describes it. That doesn't describe it. Anyway, then, in our tradition, you would play, on this instrument you didn't know how to play, you would play a song, something like a song, your love call, so to speak, so that your intended could hear the sound of your desire, untutored and new, unpracticed, authentic, poor, true. And then she would try to sing along to whatever awful noise was being made. It all makes a kind of sense, if you have a feeling for what makes people tick, and not tick. Spring nights, when the frogs are beginning to thaw, and everyone is falling in love, our little part of creation sounds like the happiest, worst orchestra in the world, tuning up. The women, often women, usually women, would lean out the windows and try to make mistakes in perfect time with their men. And this is how life went on. How the species noisily stayed a species. Joy, eternal – until the mating season ended. And after that, it was all downhill, but it felt like all uphill, but in reality, in another reality, it was probably flat, probably just a different kind of joyous. Lauren and I saw eye to eye for a while, but we were not to be, so I went my separate ways.

But, God. Our feelings, back there, back home, what a racket they made. All those rented instruments and leaning women. I miss it. You must have it here, some similar, I don't know, a similar pageantry and din. Not in my experience, but my experience here is very limited. Probably you have something else that works fine. It does seem quiet, though. I haven't noticed a lot of wailing or keening or screaming, around here. Maybe I've fallen in with the wrong crowd. *(Very brief pause.)* I don't mean you, I mean, in real life.

Sorry, if I'm…yeah.

We were taught not to talk about love. In fact, while we were indoors, we were encouraged to keep quiet on a whole range of topics. We had some different ideas about human life and the rearing of it, but we liked to think, at the very least, that our eyes were open. Which they often were. Although, I could be imagining things. Maybe I'm just imagining we had traditions and ways of life. But I don't think I am. I believe my life happened. I'm thinking of a night in the cemetery with Lauren. Her teeth in the moonlight, a pebble pressed into her elbow, all that dewy actuality. Our eyes were open. I like the little narrow roads they have in there. All the old names that look so old they seem foreign. Lauren smiled. No birds, quiet moon. True story.

But, don't get the wrong idea. We weren't all muddy skies and weeping and fornicating in the gravel. We were good at sports. Or, not sports, exactly. But, we had a national bird and special days when everything was closed. I think every country has a Memorial Day, has War Dead to honor, or some bright moment when the nation was born. Ours fell in September, and the custom was you had to make bread for anyone who asked. We were a good people, us. I like to think I'm a good person. I mean, not deep down.

We used to always…yeah, I'm sure we used to always do something. *(Brief pause. To someone in the audience.)* Sorry. I thought I saw a look in your eyes and started thinking.

I'm sorry – you can't believe how far away I feel. The answer is far. Count yourself lucky to have a safe and warm Point A somewhere in your past. I imagine myself striking out into the world, one foot in the grave, the other in my mouth, and how's anyone supposed to walk like that? Or, I imagine myself with my reading glasses resting on my forehead, as I travel the world, continent after continent, storming through cities and fields, looking for my glasses. I think that's very human of me. Near-sighted in one country is near-sighted in the next. I don't know how I imagine myself, honestly. Maybe slightly taller, with different insides. Or swinging in a hammock, on a little piece of land, without heart trouble of any kind.

But, again, I sound so dour, and I'm not. I mean, look at me. *(Brief pause, in which he stands still.)* Thanks. But, no, I knew how to unwind, back home. In fact, I could unwind almost completely. I'd chew on a piece of pine fruit and stare at the stars, almost completely unwound. Or I'd sit behind the house and try to hyperventilate or throw my bike down a hill or draw my veins on my arms and legs. I kept busy, is my point. It wasn't all scarring, back when the days weren't as numbered and bedtime was for pretending to sleep. I had a pony, almost, twice, and there was always a roof over my head to go up and sit on. And, you probably wouldn't believe it to look at me, but there'd even be the odd night when I'd enjoy a warm skipplejick. *(Brief pause, waiting for a response.)* Do you not call them that here? The point is, I'm not here to complain. I'm merely noting differences, registering differences, in an effort to draw my blurry homeland into a little more focus, so that I might decide to homesickly set sail, or happily stay put here forever. Maybe you're at a similar point in your trajectory. On the transom, or at a fork in the road, right in the middle of the tail end of a little lucky streak. That's an odd euphemism for the life span, trajectory, but it has the right connotations, the human-cannonball feel at the beginning, the sickening thump at the end. Good morning, world; maybe I should be a veterinarian or an oceanographer; maybe I'll marry a princess; thump.

But, what else? In terms of facts. Who else? I'm shooting for the essential, here. Mothers and Fathers? Those are something we probably share. We bury our mothers and fathers with tears in our eyes, back home. This is universal, I think, the burying, and fairly common, the tears. My ma and pa were sometimes known…wait. *(He opens and closes his mouth several times.)* Sorry, did you hear that? My jaw is…it's making a noise. *(Opens and closes mouth.)* Did you… *(Once more.)* I guess it's gone. No, there it is. I think the words take a toll. They sort of wear you down, certain sounds, as they move past. "Past." But I wouldn't trade them for anything, words. No, actually, I would. I would, but, for what, and with whom?

So, no, it's probably not easy. To show up, as I've shown up, on your alien shore, here, with most of the holidays being different, and the few parades we share not looking the same. We, God, back there, we'd throw a parade for anything. Shortest day of the year, longest, some kid got his braces off, another kid got scratched by a cat. We were nothing, if we were not festive. Even a neighbor's domestic dispute had us dusting off the bass drum and making banners that said, "Communication is so important." I think we just loved to march and take a stab at music. And why wouldn't we. Life was essentially a parade and it would only stop to let the ambulance through.

I don't know if you've ever followed an ambulance with your mother in it. It's mainly like driving a car, and you only start to cry when they stop running red lights or turn the siren off. The whole time you're wondering, "Does this have to happen and, since it does, does it have to happen like this?" It really doesn't matter what you scream, so scream what you like, scream your head off, son. Daughter. They're ahead of you in another vehicle and can't hear you anyway.

I once was…nah, I probably never was. I probably never was. *(Brief pause.)* What a moment, I suddenly seem to have here, with you. Standing here, a homesick orphan fuck, with no map, compass, food, bed, love. No, I don't suppose it's very easy for me. Nor for you. Alas, you know. God's wounds. And is this the part where I suddenly say, "you know, we're not that different, you and I"? I don't think so. It's probably where I say: if you have nothing good in your heart, as I don't, and nothing good in your head, as I don't, then it doesn't matter if you're out in the back yard or across the coldest ocean, you are and will always be, away from home, not at home. Not homeless, per se, necessarily, but, un-homed. Made-up word. What word isn't. Not important. People give them a hard time, but, words are fine, as said earlier, they do the trick. "My horse is sick." "Hand me that lamp." I make these sounds and someone understands, someone comprehends, and they hand me a lamp or destroy my horse. Which is a miracle, sense and meaning, feeling, that we get across even a tenth of it. And, I'm not even from here. Though we all share an origin that is, essentially, wordless. Prior to the flood and the word "flood." We all come from blood and salt water and a screaming mother begging for us to leave. And this must be an early piece of learning, something we carry with us for all time, eternal, that our arrival here caused a terrible and unsayable pain, such that all that any of the participants in that miraculous moment could do was scream. Just scream and scream, no words in sight, nothing to put a period on. No, there was nothing on the walls of the hospital where I was born. None of the advertising or posters about choking that you've got. There was a mirror, though, in the birthing room. I swear I remember it. The industrial floor tile and the whole interior. The doctor said, “It’s a boy.” There’s a way of saying that, where, depending on the delivery, it can sound more like a diagnosis than a piece of news. And then, there was this moment, maybe even caught in the mirror, of silence and peace, just mother and child and sunlight, where I swear the whole thing could be sensed, the plain truth, that this is not forever, no part of this is for forever, and all we had to do, after we’d dutifully done our screaming, all we humans in that room had to do, to begin an endless series of endings and departures and emigrations and amazement, was keep breathing. In and out, for as long as we could. The light was just right, for a moment like that. Slanty and golden. My mother said, “There, there,” and, in retrospect, she was probably right. It wasn’t a sad or dark or downward moment, it was just very heavily true. Then my father walked in with a balloon, though this I only know from a photograph. They were good people, them, but they're dead to me now, both having died. The father first, as nature would have it, and the mother later and in greater pain, and is that, again, as nature would have it? Poor women. It just doesn't stop, does it? Bleeding and bleeding and then that stops and it's "Goodnight Irene," if your name is Irene and it's night when you die. There's something sadder about a woman dying than a man. There's something sad about it all, about both. I just happen to have gotten most of my shelter from the former, so any tenderness tends in that direction.

(Brief pause.) What's that stuff you serve on salad, here? I've never seen it before. Some kind of root or something? I just was looking

through a window at a woman who had a pile of whatever it is on her plate. She touched it with a fork and tried to smile. They came by and took the other silverware away. I don't know if there was music playing.

Yeah, sorry, but, I don't sense much joy, around here, with all of you. Maybe it's there, and I don't know how to read it. Maybe it's all you feel, and I can only see it as something else.

But, again, I don't mean to judge. I'm just very far from the comforting things, as you may be. And in this state, as you may know, you can see with some precision the long straight line. All of us marching out of the ocean, breathing and breathing and breathing, and then dropping dead on land, on some land we like to mistakenly think of as ours. Thank

God, I guess, that we invented words to huff and puff, to give the whole thing some shape. There's a school of thought that says loneliness evolved sometime around the larynx, not long after the thumb. Maybe it's no surprise there isn't more smiling, but I still find it surprising.

(Pause. Looks around in audience for a smile. Finds one.) There we go. Very nice. Don't ever change. Or, if you like, change.

When I got here, about two months ago in human months, I fell in with a family, name of Miller. He did construction; she, a nurse; the girl was in school; and the boy, barely an infant, just cried and cried, and who would hold it against him, other than his parents or anyone else with a problem with littleness. They were smiley people. You could call them one of my chances. The arrangement was I'd help out around the house, but I didn't, so they asked me to leave, and I left, goodbye to the Millers. They taught me important lessons, in that brief time, mainly lessons about how to live with the Millers, but I hope to somehow extrapolate. I won't soon forget them, unless I'm thinking of the Muellers, who I didn't like at all. No, it was the Millers, and they were wonderful people. They took me in and tried to make me feel at home, having never been there, but at least they took guesses. One night, I came home and there was a tree branch in my bed. Don't know what that meant, exactly, but I'm sure it's a meaningful tribute somewhere. It's a shame. I wasn't a gracious guest, and I'm sure this deprived them of their chance to be gracious hosts. Although, I did cut my foot on a rusty metal stair, the morning I was leaving, and they tried to be understanding and said I should clean it.

I don't know if my voice sounds funny? I was using it a lot, last night. Screaming at traffic, or something. Or it might be allergies. And I wasn't really raised to speak indoors. Causation – go figure it. And I probably haven't been sleeping. Not to fall back on a favorite refrain, but: who knows. *(To a woman.)* You look like you might. Maybe? All right.

I've had occasion – this is embarrassing – to question my existence, just the plainest fact of it. Not in big ways, just little constant daily ones. This might be something the folks instilled in me. Bless their hearts, they loved me like only they could: out of the corners of their eyes, kind of, and with penetrating questions like, "Who exactly do you think you are?" and "And now where do you think you're going?" I miss my mom and dad, whoever I am, whatever's wrong with me.

But the Millers were nice. They seemed very much "from here." Just very solidly present. Which is all I'm really aiming for, right now. And so questions of here or there are hardly the point, except to further define the notion of the present moment, and actual life, as we do and don't know it, and so my problem of having one foot somewhere and the other somewhere else is really neither here nor there and should only be seen as the identification of two distant points, so as to triangulate a third and more vivid possibility. You could call this an existential crisis or dilemma, but it's really more just that my stomach hurts and I want someone to put their hand on my neck and say, "It'll be all right. We'll get you home."

No, I'm okay.

(Brief pause.) I should have brought water. My throat's drying out.

(Brief pause.) I met a blonde woman, the other – I don't know – the other week. She was from here, like yourselves. From this, this sounds so sexual, vicinity. She had a pretty way of cringing and nice blue eyes. She worked with the deaf. I found that interesting. Sometimes, she'd bring them a kitten. When I asked her why, she said, "They're cute." She was good for the world. Her life…well, I guess the word would be value, her life has value. It counts.

The world. I have these things, these words I return to. The world, women, animals, men, heart defects, disabilities, trying. My themes. The syllables I return and return to. "So, you like repeating yourself?" you say.

"I like repeating myself," I say. Because, you know, who else is going to do it? Who else is going to ride my personality into the ground and wring the last ounce of words out of my head? Others? Yeah, that's true, actually – I guess others could do it. But that doesn't mean I shouldn't try to get the most out of the old girl, which is how I refer to my body, strangely. I don't, really, I guess. But I don't call it a Him, either. It's an it, as yours is. Think, for instance, of Leonardo da Vinci or Joan of Arc. Think of Genghis Khan, or Novak Djokovic. Think of all the bodies, the muscled and rippled and lithesome Its that once strode the wonderful Earth, sailed the seventy seas, coughing and wheezing and theorizing and sinking. The magnificent Its, come and gone, neither hither nor yon. It's exciting, isn't it. Being a part of the great

Hide-and-Seek? The great swarm, the living billions, as we try to get our footing, place ourselves in some continuum, before the lights go out and the thing discontinues. It's exciting, if nothing else. Now you see us, oh my God I can't breathe, now you don't. And then we're all by the grave in the rain, dreaming of breakfast. "He was a good man, even a family man, in his way. But, not anymore. Now he's in a coffin, or across the river, or in the clouds. And wherever he is, we pray his soul might find repose, that it might find rest, somewhere, at least for a while, if not for ever and ever, Amen."

(Brief pause.) That was a eulogy. Everything is, if you have a good sense of humor, a positive mindset. I mean that. If you have the right attitude, the right kind of bright and cheerful approach, the whole fucking swill-hole is just a

long line of informative and beautiful funerals. Here comes one now. I can almost see it, as it disappears. *(He closes his eyes.)* The steam rising off the sweating horses in the winter weather. Their breath, visible. The quiet, the sound of wooden cart wheels on a cobbled road. You, in tears, or dead. The smell of worms and roots, the smell of cold air. *(He opens his eyes.)* Can you picture it? Something close? Something ceremonious? Flowers and dirt and the whole crying family. The landscapers smoking. The folding of the death rug and a bottle of pine sap broken over the coffin. The speechlessness. The survivor's veiny hands.

I'm describing my own, how we have them back home. Hence the horses and cobblestone, which, when I think of it, we don't have anymore. I'm also describing it from the perspective of the living. Which is how we tend to see everything. We're very living-oriented, aren't we. This is how a funeral might seem to the deceased. *(He holds a long, tense, pause. Mumbles something urgently but quietly, indecipherably. Then, a very quiet but menacing drone. Then one small sad sound.)* *(Brief pause.)* No, that's probably not right. *(Brief pause.)* We have a tradition, where I hail from, of crying. Late at night, broad daylight, whenever we have a moment. I'm sure you do too. But, we really made a name for ourselves with it. But I swear that I am, like you, not unhappy.

(Brief pause.) We should thank our stars, if we believe in stars, for the listeners of the world. You're doing fine, is what I'm saying. You're doing very well and I thank you.

The blonde woman had a nice name: Lisa. It's good, yeah? It doesn't really preen, as a name. Lisa, you remember, from the vicinity? She tried to take me to a Trivia Night, for a taste of the local culture. It was a good idea, but we went on the wrong night. Do you know what night is Trivia Night at the Whately Cafe? Wednesday, the correct answer is Wednesday. But so we walked around for a while. It was cold and supposed to snow. So that was something we shared, that it was supposed to snow.

You don't see much ice or snow where I'm from. I do have a story, though, a sighting. I could never sleep, whatever year I'm thinking of, and so was out, at some ungodly hour, on some bastardly late winter night, taking my walk. It was only me, or farmers, or escapees or hunters, who were out in the very cold dark. I could hear that thundery sound I was always hearing, although it sounded more metallic. I stopped to turn around and then turned around again. And then I saw the sight it seemed I was born to see, if I was born for a reason. The scene was this, in words, it was about a hundred just-shorn sheep, shorn too early in the season, standing dead still, all facing the same way, with a couple of skinny cows mixed in, standing as still as the sheep, and then the snow beginning to slowly fall. Silent scrawny creatures in the slow-motion snow, a communal shiver that would make its way through the crowd, an occasional animal vowel sound, and that was quietly all, that was quietly that.

It was there, standing before all them huddled against the weather, that I decided to leave, for real and for good, and not just in my heart.

And not just leave there, but try to actually go somewhere. I thought, "Maybe I've been adapting to the wrong surroundings." It wasn't a moment I fully understood, though there was definitely a strain of hope in it. Maybe another decade or two went by, and, ta-da. Je suis arrivé. That's French. Or, according to earlier claims, it's a eulogy. If everything is. I guess "Here we are" announces the death of our having been somewhere else. Who knows, again, and so on. The leafless trees, against the winter sky. The breath, visible. And so on. Words are all right. You say what you want, at the end of the day, they somehow work their magic. "Please stay seated." *(Very brief pause. No one has moved.)* See? Thank you. Well done. "Remain forever lost, ye beautiful and crooked people, wandering in the wilderness of doubt." *(Very brief pause.)* Again, wow, well done. Very nicely done.

Electricity, let's talk about that. It varies. Different regions, different plugs and voltages. Let's not talk about that. Let's try to stick to the things that don't vary. But what doesn't vary?

(Brief pause.) I wasn't breast-fed. So I didn't really know what to reach for or something. Maybe I should've said that, at the beginning. I found my mother's diary, is how I know, although I also had a feeling, if that's what that was. The top of the baby bottle I originally drank from got lost at some point, the part with the rubber nipple, so I, apparently, would kind of lap the baby-formula from this wide-mouthed pickle jar they'd put near me on the ground. It was a sight, my mother wrote, that, quote, "did not fill anyone with much pride." There's a later entry about my father not being very happy about my teeth

coming in. Something about him not liking the consonant sounds I started making. The same day he said that, we, reportedly, drove somewhere to look at a dining room table someone was giving away. I was in the back seat, looking out the window, staring fearfully at the world and smiling, reportedly.

Somebody told me, I think it was a nutritionist I met, that you have to have a bicycle when you're little. That it's the law here. That can't be true, can it? True or false, it's a beautiful idea. *(To the audience in general.)* Remember, that night, years ago, when you were a beautiful idea? When you were just a glint and a smirk and an unspecified word? *(Very brief pause.)* Of course not – you weren't there. Except in spirit. In the spirit of a word or a smirk.

Lisa and I were going to rent a tandem once. It was just that kind of day. Lisa, I've mentioned her a few times now, she of the blondeur. I had the wrong identification or something, so they wouldn't let us take one, but we watched everyone else. I remember, there was a mother with her daughter, in unmatching outfits, trying to patch things up somehow, wobbling off together. Lisa looked disappointed but pretty, sitting there watching. I just remembered this: bangs. Bangs? That's some thing with how you wear your hair, yeah? I'd never heard that until I heard it from her. She was an education, our Lisa. One time, we went to a flea market and she told me, "Don't get too lost for too long," while she was flipping through some used post cards. That was a good day.

I think she couldn't handle the distance. I mean, the distance of me, or something. She asked me, very innocently, what I was doing on Earth. She said, "It's all right, if you're not sure." She straightened my collar and said, "You look like you just got born. Most people get over that. I could hold you," she said. I remember because it was memorable. "I could hold you." She would've been a good person to tremble with. But I got stupid and cold, and probably left her no choice. She was sweet when she ended it. She said, "You're really not where I see myself in five years." I don't know if she worked on that for days or just said it off the top of her head. I had hopes that we, that she and I... I just thought we'd exist for a while. She dropped off some things I'd left at her house, along with a calendar with all the days we'd spent together blacked out. Is that something people do? Is there something people don't? You know? It's such a range.

I'd like to think it was her loss, but sometimes it's hard to tell which loss is whose. I never really knew where I stood, with Lisa and everyone and all that.

The fucking world. I'm sorry, but, the fucking earth. Time, place, happiness. A person should be able to figure it out. It's only three things. Where did Philosophy go? Or Religion? We've had ten thousand years of people telling us what life is and how best to live it as it quickly goes by. And what has it given us? Me? I hope not. I don't know. Maybe homesickness and seasickness are the new and improved way of feeling at home. Or, maybe…just, anything.

God, water. *(Brief pause.)* They say to touch the roof of your mouth with your tongue.

(Brief pause, as he does so.) It's just a bad patch. I'm all right. I'm not feeling anything you haven't felt. It's like, you know, when they have you gargle with the sand for your second birthday. *(He turns away, momentarily, sees his bag. He gets the old metal lunchbox out of the bag.)* This'll offer us a little diversion. A little breather. My other belonging. Now, this object tells an interesting story. *(He holds it up for a moment.)* Not in words, I guess. *(He opens it. It's empty.)* Ah. The universe provides. I mean it. There's room to put something in there. *(Sets it down or puts it back in the bag, somewhere in the next few lines.)* I travel light. Or I don't have very much. By way of explanation.

(Referring to any piece of jewelry or any kind of accessory that someone in the audience is wearing.) I'm noticing your thing, there.

Where I'm from, at least in the western part, you have a birth cloud. They take you out the day you're born, the day after, and you all look up, and you pick a cloud, and if some uncle has a camera he takes a picture, and that's your birth cloud, and there you are. In the old days, they used to do a drawing. Good tradition, The Birth Cloud. It was to remind us, I guess, of what happens, eventually. It was nice, whatever it meant, a comfort, whatever the ancient roots. I'm sure you have something similar, here. I know you have the Birth Stone. That's obviously very different, but somehow a similar statement is being made. "You're a deaf and mute block of matter" or, "You're drifting by and slowly disappearing." Something like that. A little fact to put around the child's neck to guide him or her in his or her behavior.

(Without making any sounds, he opens and closes his mouth several times.) Sorry, again, but, you must hear that? No? Sorry. I grind my teeth in my sleep. I guess I grind them when I'm up, too.

(Brief pause.) I don't have a relative anywhere on this continent. Maybe you find that comforting.

(He works his mouth, for just a second, perhaps gags, for a second.) This doesn't feel good. But, we came here to get somewhere.

We actually have a word, "somewhere." And a word, "nowhere." We have a word, "tree," too, but you can actually picture that. I guess there was a need. I guess it was important we had names for places, even if we didn't have the places.

(Brief pause.) Before my father died, he didn't have a lot left of the gifts that you, again, thank you kindly and sincerely, are currently lavishing on me. Meaning, mainly, hearing and seeing. I'd say, "You want some cheese and crackers?" and he'd say, "Watch your mouth." So I'd say: *(Mumbles an indecipherable short sentence, something like: "Get your own fucking lunch," but indecipherable.)* In the end, his world was just a room, and a window, and the walk out to the mailbox. The world gets very small, doesn't it, penultimately. I wasn't by his side or anything, at the exact moment. I'm told he had no last words, just some different sounds. I was asleep, or just waking up. Time Zones, you know. And so ended his great journey, reportedly.

Lavishing is the word. I do thank you.

(Somewhere in the following lines a very gentle and imperceptible light shift should begin to occur, resulting in the "nice glow" that's referred to in the end.) I made it back for my mother's, though. The words very close to her dying words were "How is Catherine?" I think she thought I was her cousin. "Was there any traffic?" she asked me. Women care more about the world, so it's bigger for them, and maybe that's why it's sadder when they die. My mother said, "Tell them not to have a parade," because she never liked the mess. Then she said, "I can see you." She put her hands in front of her face. "Where's the little person?" And then she said, "Flowers would've brightened things up." And then her breathing changed and then because of fluid that had built up, or, just, it doesn't matter why, just, suddenly, she wasn't, I don't know how to say

it, she wasn't my mother anymore. But she still was. Her breathing got very raspy, or, some adjective. She died, would be the most economical way to put it. Where do you look, in the room? Where do you stand? No corner is corner enough, in certain rooms.

(Brief pause.) I'm sorry. We've all lost someone, I'm sure, someone who held us down to earth somehow or pointed us off in the right direction. I say this gently, and maybe it's just the light, but, God, we all look like we've got barely anyone left. *(Very brief pause.)* I'm sorry about that. All those losses. Each with its own, I don't know, dimensions? Co-ordinates? It's disorienting. What do you do. Where do you turn.

(A little lost in a sad and painful reverie of loss, he takes out the three-foot piece of broomstick.)

This is made out of electrons. Ash, actually. I think it's ash. I've kept it all these years. *(He gently taps several times the side of his lower leg. Then he strikes his leg very hard, "whack.")* Hey, still works. *(He hits himself again, twice, and then, again, several more times. Perhaps in tears.)* That's for the things I don't know. That's for all the places. *(Another whack or two.)* The old song and dance. The old girl. I'm sorry.

(Long pause. He regains a kind of raw but simple composure.) I've gotten sidetracked. I was talking about travel and how it started with my mother and father. They brought me into this world, of course, and taught me the difference between right and left. They taught me the word home, the word walk. *(He looks at someone in the audience. Gently.)* What's that look? *(Very brief pause.)* No, it's nice.

I had wanted to leave you with something. *(Very brief pause. Seeming to respond to an audience member's anxiety.)* I know, I know, time, of course – I'm sure we all have somewhere we're supposed to be. *(Brief pause.)* There's a nice little glow, here. Is that…am I seeing that right? It's sort of morning-like? Late morning?

Don't get too lost for too long. They stop looking, eventually. Then even you forget you were ever out here somewhere.

(Another brief moment of difficulty, with breathing, swallowing, the jaw, etc.) This might be a good place to stop. Here.

It's a funny thing, it's strange – thirst, or whatever this is. Being a person. All the needs, the feelings, all the different things arising, thoughts. *(Lights begin a five second fade.)* The Earth.

End.

OH, THE HUMANITY

and other good intentions

Oh, the Humanity and other good intentions was first produced at the Flea Theater, New York, on 3 November 2007, with the following cast:

Marisa Tomei

Brian Hutchison

Drew Hildebrand

Directed by Jim Simpson

Sets by Kyle Chepulis

Lighting by Brian Aldous

Costumes by Claudia Brown

Sound by Jill B C DuBoff

Video/projection by Dustin O'Neill

First produced in the UK, by special arrangement with SUBIAS, at Northern Stage, Newcastle upon Tyne, on 9 September 2011 with the following cast:

Tony Bell

Lucy Ellinson

John Kirk

Directed by Erica Whyman

Designed by Andrew Stephenson

Lighting Design by Kevin Tweedy

Composition by Leif Jordansson

Sound Design by Rob Brown

Dialect Coach Michaela Kennen

The author, who is mainly American, and who might not be an author but for the following, would like to thank the following, who are mainly English: Jack Bradley, Chris Campbell, Daisy Heath, Gordon Lish, Paul Miller, Joe Sola, Kester Thompson, and Erica Whyman.

BEHOLD THE COACH, IN A BLAZER, UNINSURED

Dramatis Persona

THE COACH

Setting

A press conference. A table with a paper cup and several microphones on it.

THE COACH

He enters, places his keys, cigarettes, etc, on the table. Sits down.

All right, everybody, let's just get going. You people know what I've come here to probably say. This should all come as all as no surprise. The phrase, of course, you are familiar with. It was a "building year," this last year was. We suffered some losses, yes, we suffered some, last season, and we had to start out all over, in a fashion; we had to come at this thing as if it were a—you folks in the press can tell me if this is a pleonasm—a new beginning. We made some changes here and there and here and we made these, mainly, mostly, with the fans in mind, because we wanted the fans to be happy, in our minds we wanted the fans to love us. And I think they should be happy, in my mind I think they should love us.

Listen, last year was not the easiest year. The plan was that it would be for building, for rebuilding, for replacing what was lost, replenishing what was gone, and trying to reverse a routine of losing that had grown in-grown and somehow strangely proud. Our strategy was, in theory, to betray that which had become merely habit, to betray our very fear, the very thing that's kept us alive, the thing that says to us: Don't cross the street without looking both ways first; Don't speak your mind and certainly never your heart.

Brief pause.

But habit's a hard habit to break.

Brief pause.

And was it only habit that kept us from dropping to our knees in the middle of the street and sobbing and begging "Can somebody help me, please?" Was it just mere routine that kept us on our feet, with our mouths shut and our hands in our pockets?

One night, after practice—some of you might appreciate this—I found myself standing in the unforgivable light of a grocery store, staring at my reflection in a freezer, and realizing: "You're not having a bad day—this is just what you look like, now. This is who the years are making you." The praying kind probably would have prayed. I just wanted to grab a courtesy phone and beg into it: "Could someone come to the front of the store and clean up the spill that is my life on this earth? Could somebody please just somehow help me through this punishing crushing nauseating sorrow?"

Brief pause.

So that's what this last year was. We had to look hard at a few things and, surprise surprise, we found that they looked hard back. But in many ways, I think we have to be happy. We sold some hot dogs. We got some sun, some fresh air. We played some close games—some of them, even, we were still in until right up to the end. It was the life, it really was, and, granted, yeah, no, this was not the greatest year. Some people are saying it was barely even a shambles. I'm sure there's a more charitable view, but, okay: fair enough. Fair enough.

Brief pause.

I had no idea how hard hard was until this year came around. Nights, whole nights, weeks of nights, in a row. I bet I walked a thousand miles up and down my street alone. I came home and went out, walking. My eyes all runny, just walking, counting up the things I don't have anymore, thinking of the Fair Lady of my own incompetent sonnets. Who I lost, by the way. Or, failed to win. Or, forfeited, in some miserable show of inwardness, or downwardness, or shame.

Brief pause.

It was a hard year. Tough schedule.

Brief pause.

My love is like a sunset, stunning, and then over.
And in the year since her, there has not been
A single thing but ashes and formalities.
A year of cigarette butts and minor car crashes.
Rosemary, for remembrance;
Glucosamine and Chondroitin, for the joints.
And I will never love
any thing or body again.
And I am not young and handsome.
And I could not coach a gallon of water
Out of a paper bag.

Pause.

So. That was some poetry. And, so, yes, obviously, I've had my doubts. I've had what you people might call Personal Problems. But I tried. To run things different. With a little elegance, a new uniform. I tried writing that thing about the sunset. I tried to act with some sense of honor and calm amidst the urgency and vulgarity of the—I don't know. You tell me, you lived through it, too, you lived right straight through it, too. What was this year? Can we even—I don't know. Christ Jesus Christ.

He directs the question toward a person in the audience.

What did you feel, this past year? Of what would you be speaking, if you were sitting here, this year, speaking of the last? And did any one of us have what he would call a winning season? And what would that even look like? And could someone tell me, while we're at it, when is High School over, when comes High School to its high-schoolish end? When begins my true life as me on Earth? Because I really don't understand when the seriousness is supposed to start. And I'm so filled with wanting, I so crave to know, just a little anything, a fact, a meaning, a song, even a jingle. A little lullaby, to be put to sleep by, to sleep. I'd like to know a real poem. By someone other than me, with a vocabulary other than mine. Just a gentle little rhymey poem for the old boy with the clipboard and whistle.

Pause.

It was a real hell of a hell of a time, this year. What's that saying? About the penguin? And the fifty-yard dash? Well, that's exactly what it was. Really.

Brief pause.

It was a trying time. A building year. An endless gorgeous gorgeous endless loss. Which now is now over. And we have how many more left left to us to lose?

Pause.

Now, I know you guys in the press are going to have a field day with some of the things I've said up here today.

He stands.

And I know you're probably thinking: Something seems to have kind of snuffed out the fire this guy had when we hired him. You're probably thinking: Could someone in this condition ever get it all together and grab it with both hands and win us a championship, given the fact that he's halfway-gone in distraction and mourning for a woman who was solely herself in every inch of her body and might have been the best thing that ever happened to him, assuming he's even capable of letting someone happen to him? Could someone like this ever show us how not to lose? Well, I'll tell you, because I came here to tell you a few things. I came here to feel the burn from your flash bulbs, and to speak a few things into that harsh light, my heart included. And the answer is, I don't know. I don't know if I can lead anyone to victory, or even lead anyone anywhere. I don't know if my plan is a good one, or even if I have one.

I am asking you to just let me be still. To let me turn my face upward to the heavens, while the rest of me slumps earthward, and let me say, you've got to please just hear me and let me stand here and say, to the sky, or the ceiling, and to all of you, and I quote:

Brief pause.

I don't know. In general. And, in particular, in particular.

All I know is that someone has to be everywhere. And I—it's hard not to realize—I am the one who is up here, now. Before all of you who are sitting there, there. I am the one in the position I'm in. I stand before you, as that man. In spite of all the grim realities and lonely terms of this great game and all that we who play it face. And I lived as that man through this last year, past. And I think I should be happy. I do. I think we should all be very terribly proud and happy, and happy and afraid, and afraid and thrilled, really thrilled to death at the upcoming year and all of the life it will naturally contain.

This is my feeling on this.

We probably only have time for one question.

Blackout.

END

LADIES AND GENTLEMEN, THE RAIN

Dramatis Personae

GENTLEMAN

LADY

Setting

Each of the characters is recording a video, for the purpose of employing a dating service.

General notes concerning staging

Each of the characters is seated on a stool, the LADY at stage left, the GENTLEMAN at stage right. Two cameras are set on tripods before them (these can also simply be implied). Though there is no physical barrier between them, the two never regard one another, and never acknowledge the presence of the other's body on stage, except perhaps, at times, in a very subliminal way. At certain times, they stand, preen, move forward or walk around to behind their chairs, for the point of emphasis.

GENTLEMAN and LADY, in low light, are seated as described above. The two are straightening a collar, smoothing a dress, generally preparing to be on camera. Lights up.

LADY

Is it started? Are we started? I'll wait.

GENTLEMAN

Hi. I'm a little nervous. Who isn't? Anyway. Where to begin. I guess there's no need for me to try describing myself, since, well, here I am, here. I look like this. I don't know whether that's good news. But, okay, what else? I'm good at grocery shopping. Fairly good. I shine my own shoes. I don't try to say anything funny when someone close has died. I don't stop drinking. I know women have their times. I'm average-sized. Of average intelligence. Blood pressure, too, I guess.

LADY

Sorry—now? Sorry.

GENTLEMAN

No pets, but, I have a great love and understanding of the dog. Although almost none of any other animal. For instance, once some geese came flying over me and I thought, "Now where the hell are they going?" Another time, a moth was bothering me by flying at my lamp. So I turned it off. A third animal incident concerns a mourning dove, and how quick I was to make it wish that we had never met.

He pauses.

I'm hardly ever like that.

LADY

Looking into the light.

I can't tell if there's anyone… I guess I'll just start talking. I love the outdoors. Air and weather, the sky. I'm the type to like walking around, with the little book, trying to identify trees or plants. I like it indoors, too, don't get me wrong, The Great Indoors. But I love being outside. I like swimming. I have five bathing suits. No, four, because one time I was—no, I was right, it's five. It's not important.

Brief pause.

I never saw myself doing this. I've seen myself doing things, strangely. But not this.

Brief pause.

Anyway. Feelings, me, thoughts. I'm always surprised when the ocean gets really quiet. And I don't get why breaking the sound barrier should make so much noise. Things like that. Everything seems too quiet or too loud. I'm torn exactly in half, about fifty per cent of the time. This is most days. Although, other times, things aren't quite so clear. For instance, once, I couldn't get over it, but there it was, and you go figure it out.

GENTLEMAN

I have different interests. I enjoy not traveling. I don't speak any second language. Fine dining, live music, and cinema can come and go. I stay out of museums. I stay away from home. I don't have a favorite food, but I guess I like cholesterol. I tend not to speak unless spoken to. In the summer, I like not having the heat on. In the winter, I like to not sit in front of a fan. I try to look on the bright side. I am not, as I look around myself, currently bleeding.

LADY

I'm one of those people who believes there are two kinds of people. And these can be divided into billions of other kinds of people, which time prohibits me from, you know, I don't know… But I have my type. My types, I guess. I like watching people clapping for something they really like, and, watching someone sign his signature. I'm also attracted to men who black out when asked a difficult question. (*A small quick smile.*) I guess I mean I like it when I feel I'm really being heard.

GENTLEMAN

When I was little, I…wait. God. Weird. I forget what I was going to say. "When I was little." It's completely gone.

LADY

Dislikes? Rudeness. Untimely remarks. Bossy…bossiness. Ostentation. Also, nerve damage and heart disease. Heat stroke, also. Heat death. Regular people death. The dying of U.S. presidents. The death of a family dog. Alice, for instance. The passing of eras, decades, everything, all this time going by, getting old, dying, in a sense. Like grass. Like annual flowers. Like something, like that. Like people.

She pauses.

None of that really puts me in the mood. But I guess there's a chance that any of it could.

GENTLEMAN

While LADY has been speaking, he has been trying to remember the thing he forgot. He decides to move on, shakes his head, almost imperceptibly.

GENTLEMAN *(Cont'd)*

Anyway. Onward. I am such a fan of shoulder-length hair. And any color eyes. And I like how women talk. I have faults, obviously. Some weak points are my knees and back. And I don't have any patience for things that take a long time. Although, it should be said, I'm usually very deeply just waiting. Bugs fly in my mouth sometimes, because I'm just standing there, full of want, full of open-mouthed wonder. I stay like that long enough to give them time to fly out, because, although unknowing, I am not unkind.

Brief pause.

I like walking. I'll run, if I have to. Or stay still. But you're never going to find me shaking on the floor, biting into my own hand, and crying out into the daylight. Except, sometimes. But really only rarely, on those occasions.

LADY

Give life a go with this attractive and elegant woman. This sensitive and sympathetic, maybe somewhat removed, I don't know, somewhat ingoing, but, sensitive, sympathetic…

GENTLEMAN

See the world. See the—I don't know—world. See some sort of…

LADY

You know what,—

GENTLEMAN

Did you ever feel—

LADY

I don't know. God. Sometimes,…

GENTLEMAN

Sometimes, I just want to do someone over and have that be it. Sometimes, I—quote—love, with nothing but my hands and the dried-out words I've practiced and remembered. Quote love.

LADY

A lot of times, it's only to somehow make someone pay for my former life as a child. A lot of times I don't feel anything but the come on my stomach.

GENTLEMAN

"I'm not what I look like," I want to say to people who think I look like a certain kind of person. Even though, when I think about it, I see how I could be wrong.

LADY

I'm sorry. Sometimes I feel differently. Sometimes, I find the world so, I don't know, so attractive, and I look at it, the world, and I think of all the different parts of it, all the people and things that can happen, and I think, Wow. Ouch. But mainly, Wow.

GENTLEMAN

I take it back. Forget what I just said.

LADY

What else is a person supposed to say?

GENTLEMAN

Who doesn't have a few bad days, out of the twenty-five thousand? The twenty thousand?

LADY

She glances at a piece of paper, obviously something she's prepared in advance:

"Hear the call of the evening, of the night, of a lone person, the call of a trembling paragraph of speech, of my favorite language, English."

Brief pause.

It was my minor.

GENTLEMAN

This is from a thing that I, I don't know…

He reads:

"Let's go out, into the night, into rancor, over shiny highways, down grand canyons and tree-lined dead-ends, milady and I, into and unto the rude world awaiting." It's from this letter I tried writing.

LADY

I want to start a family. Or, at least, finish one. Either way, that would be later. What else can I tell you? "You."

Brief pause.

I like wine. Summer. Same as anyone. I wear dresses. I used to know how much I weighed, soaking wet. You know that old phrase. I used to… My first…

Pause.

I have this picture. In my mind. In it, I'm soaking wet. From running and sweating and the rain or from the feeling I'm having. Everything is all—I'm sorry… I've lived with it for as long as I've lived with anything. I can see the sky. I can see the trees, bending, and the birds, flying away somewhere. And me. And I'm running, in a dress, and it's raining. There's the feeling of someone else, of some ghostly You, there or just about to be there. I'm always running. Not away from or toward, just running. And the sky keeps changing, and me underneath it. Gray, blue, white, dark gray, dark gray. I'm in a meadow, usually, near some woods, looking at everything, at all the natural forces and the leaves moving, trying to find some secret order in it, some higher darker good. Some lasting helpful truth other than that the world moves on, destroying things. Me, for example—for example, myself.

GENTLEMAN

As for yourself, you're of a sunny disposition. You have what shampoo bottles would describe as normal hair. You like seeing those plywood signs that say "Pick your own berries." Sometimes you like to cook and clean. Sometimes you don't. You're quiet in bed, unless in the middle of some great woe or, I don't know, something.

Brief pause.

Sometimes, you wish you were dead, but you'll probably die wishing you could live, and you know that. You imagine things a certain way. You draw little drawings of things. You were young. You get scared to death. You start shaking. I know you're out there, somewhere. Shaking.

LADY

You're always in the distance. Athletic, lean—or I don't know. Just *describable*, somehow. Recognizable. To me. People can see your life story in your posture, in the way you look at things and hold yourself. You probably collect something. You were once suicidal, but have since lost interest. You're looking for me. Someone like me. I've been described as The Girl Next Door, by neighbors. I'm occasionally given to crying in the daytime. I'm given to wearing no shoes. I'm given to suffering from cervical cancer, disorder in the nervous system, immense pain in my lower back, and fits of unspeakable but finally ultimately not-uncommon anguish in the night. I'm given to probably almost everything, eventually. I like horseback riding.

GENTLEMAN

I like riding horses. One time I fell. I did something to my shoulder. It healed. But I got older and older. And that kept happening. And all that time, I kept having this, I don't know—I'm not the type to have visions—but, this vision. I'm standing in your yard. In the country. I don't know how I got here. It's fall. The weather is always cold and rainy, unpromising, good. You're coming home, holding groceries, fooling with your keys, looking up. It's so simple. Notice me. Please care that I'm standing on your property, in the rain. Acknowledge my soaked clothes somehow. I want to say something, just call over to you. I just want to say, Hey, hi, it's me. After all these years.

Brief pause.

This isn't imaginary. I know it isn't. I'm looking at you and asking you, I'm not alone, right now, on Earth, right now, am I?

He whispers.

Fuck.

LADY

Isn't a life just a history of the times when you did or didn't turn? This is how I always saw it. This. With you right there, but not yet, and the clouds all dramatic. I just want you to turn. Please come toward me. Just look at me for once in my life. I'm saying Please. I'm saying Look.

GENTLEMAN

I know what happens in life. But I don't know if I'll be alone when it does. It seems like a big thing not to know.

LADY

The birds and animals and everything are all quiet.

GENTLEMAN

I picture us in a cemetery.

LADY

What a beautiful day.

GENTLEMAN

Standing under a tree. Arms touching. Our arms touching.

LADY

Just the rain dripping on the leaves. Like in every poem ever written. Just you and me, side by side.

GENTLEMAN

I just want to be calm. And to be able to look without having to look away.

LADY

I want to feel home for once. Together with someone in the regular world but also together in another little world of our own devisement. I believe in this. My picture of life. Why would I keep having it? I read the newspapers but I still believe in this.

GENTLEMAN

I feel weak. I'm worried I'm weak. I get nervous, sometimes. I don't know what to say, sometimes. Which is weak.

LADY

I've waited and waited, and, look at me, I still am. In all recorded time, what were they recording, if not the secret and sideways dreams of people like us, lone people in serious wait. Like it's what we're born for.

Brief pause.

Devisement's a word, isn't it?

GENTLEMAN

When I used to be younger, it was my belief that you met some other person. I believed that the world was small. I thought that the world was my mother and father. And then you find someone, some other person, and you just go, simple as that, you just go off somewhere, and get old slowly somewhere, in love. I believed that people were perfect. And life went on forever.

He pauses.

I was right. About everything.

LADY

I enjoy tennis.

GENTLEMAN

Please send a photograph.

LADY

A sense of humor is important.

GENTLEMAN

You could send a drawing.

LADY

I would walk all over the bleeding world—

GENTLEMAN

I'd like to see your handwriting.

LADY

—I would, for a man who would tell me the time.

GENTLEMAN

I swear I'll answer.

LADY

I'm the type of girl who likes music. And who, on Earth, is *not* the type of girl who likes music. I'm looking for someone to talk with. I'd give up my body in this world for a single conversation.

GENTLEMAN

I'm looking for someone, and I hope that I'll know her when I see her. I am looking for something that seems so far to have been happy to have kept itself hidden.

LADY

Have I said what my name was?

GENTLEMAN

Is there a little light that's supposed to come on?

Blackout, or fairly quick fade.

END

ENTER THE SPOKESWOMAN, GENTLY

Dramatis Persona

SPOKESWOMAN FOR COUNTRY AIR

Setting

A press conference. A podium, on which are mounted several microphones and the Country Air corporate logo.

SPOKESWOMAN

She enters.

Hello. First of all, let me just say that we are suffering with you families. Let me say, just, that we're suffering, we're staring at each other and up into the sky, like you, and that we have, while staring, tried to act. In a first very small step, we have as of tonight called off tomorrow's company picnic. I know that doesn't sound serious. We are canceling other events as well, because of the failure of the airplane. We don't know what we should do, honestly, or what we should say after doing it. But we do know the last thing anyone wants to see is us enjoying life, drinking too much and driving home drunk with someone from personnel, with a temporary tattoo and a sunburn. So, the picnic, of course, is off.

I have a father who died, incidentally. He taught me sports and going outside, picnic things. So I was just thinking about him. My father's gone, possibly as yours is, though mine died in a chair. He died sitting quietly, and not in a plane in flames, screaming downward at the speed of sound. His final resting place was an unraveling easy-chair in the living room. He was only human, and though it could have been, this was not listed as the cause of death. Countless nights beneath relatively fatherly men did nothing to lift the weight of that sad time. Excuse me, I'm sorry.

Brief pause.

I don't know what it would be good for you to do. Try those things we all try.

A pause.

As for why, it is, as of tonight, undetermined. Who knows? Bad weather, an act of God or some handsome pilot's drunken error? Whatever it was, here we are. And we'll try to move forward, with time, taking hard comfort in the fact that, with or without us, time is moving forward, too.

A pause.

But, so, yes—it was flight 514, the night flight to Johnston, and there were, at this time, no survivors. We have been told so little so far. Gravity, we trust, was a factor. Did they know when it was still up that it was coming down? We hope not. We hope they felt secure on their airplane, as do we on our earth, and denied the fact of their coming doom, as do we ours. We hope they were enjoying the in-flight movie. Which was a Norwegian film called *The Bleeding Parade.* I don't know if these small details are helpful.

I do have some news, or, business, some awful business. Families of the deceased get a round-trip ticket, as well as a bereavement allowance, which should help with travel and funeral plans. You get so little, sometimes. You people whose loved one is gone, you people who are, in fact, in fact, also going, dying, but from the inside out, from having time go by, as died my dad, as will probably die me, not from doing anything daring, not flying, or skydiving, just sitting there being human with your mouths open, looking so sweet and deaf. What a world, isn't it. All of us. There may be other compensation.

I want to say—I'm the spokesperson, it's my job, and it's not easy—but I want to say to you: I understand, I think I understand. You waited and waited at the airport, you raced there in the first place, through unspeakable traffic, and the parking situation, and then you got to the proper gate and waited and they didn't come and didn't come and the monitor said DELAYED and I'm sure it was confusing, and then frustrating, and now just so sad. And can these things, can any sad things, ever even be compared? Is it insulting to you if I think they can? I'm sorry. My degree was in Hospitality Management. I fell into this job through an acquaintance in the field.

A brief pause.

We're all going there, wherever, at different speeds, in different styles. I guess I am, as the spokesperson here, speaking to you, asking you to look around. Look at your hands. They used to be so tiny. Now they're not, and they're old. There are lines in our faces around our eyes from years of just laughing and using the wrong soap. The body is its own disaster area. The human face is a call for help. (*Calmly and gravely:) Help, We need help, We are in flames, Port engine out, No radio. Landing gear is mangled, Radar is blank, Please foam the runway, We are coming in, coming home and down, and so shall you all.*

A pause.

I'm sorry. We don't have a formalized tack we take in events like this. We understand how little there is to say, but that something must be said. We are grateful that nights like this are rare, that Country Air has a record of somewhat excellence—but I know that doesn't help. I want to help, but I know I can't, and I know that doesn't help. So, help me, and hear me, and understand, I beg you, that I'm just saying… Maybe it was quiet. Maybe all the lights and engines were out and it was just a dark and quiet thing falling through the night. The whole thing coming apart like a comet, but, also, unlike anything. And maybe, I'm just saying, maybe it was the high point of something, maybe it was somehow something's perfect ending. Maybe all the people in the crashing plane were thinking of you, the soon-to-be still-living, were wishing you were there, assuming useless crash positions among the blankets and little liquor bottles, living, busy, falling through the air, a silence in the silence, about to make a serious noise. Maybe they felt famous. Or special or chosen. Loved, maybe, somehow, finally. I don't know. We don't.

A pause.

This was, by the way, an experienced experienced crew. They had flown several thousands of hours. They knew what they were doing.

A pause.

We're so sorry. We wish it could have been another way, but it wasn't. We are asking you to be grateful. Here we are, that's all, just us, here, still, and we want you to see the miracle of this. Officially, we would like you to feel giddy, for your heart to pound, for you to feel blessed, that the plane stayed up for as long as it did. That the plane could even fly at all. That the thing actually got off the ground in the first place.

This is all I can currently say.

I'm so sorry.

I would tell you more if I knew more.

Lights down.

END

THE BULLY COMPOSITION

Dramatis Personae

PHOTOGRAPHER
male

ASSISTANT
female

(In the program, no roles should be listed. Only the actors' names should appear, e.g., "John Smith. Jane Jones." The reason for this is to encourage the audience to more easily accept the possibility that this is an improvisation.)

Setting

Theatre.

Stage Properties

A large-format box camera (with a flash), a tripod, a light meter, some lights. A folder full of photos and papers.

PHOTOGRAPHER and ASSISTANT enter. PHOTOGRAPHER begins to set up a camera (with a flash, perhaps some remote flash devices) and tripod, aimed at the audience. ASSISTANT has a folder filled with papers, photographs, etc. ASSISTANT looks around at the theatre and audience, checking light meter readings. Both PHOTOGRAPHER and ASSISTANT speak mainly to the audience, and do so in a very natural way that must seem extemporaneous, but in a way that should also, at times, express just as naturally an intense gravity. Any disagreements they have will be managed calmly and respectfully. Their differing views will be expressed bluntly and plainly but without intense emotions.

ASSISTANT

Don't be nervous. Just act natural.

PHOTOGRAPHER

Fidgeting with camera.

This should only take a minute.

Brief pause.

To make a record of your souls.

ASSISTANT

Don't blink.

Looking around at the light in the theater, checking a meter reading.

We may need more light. I don't know, maybe not.

Brief pause. Pulling a small antique photograph, wrapped in a protective cover, out of a folder. The photograph, though the audience won't really be able to see it, should be of a grotesquely mutilated corpse.

Anyway, why don't we start.

PHOTOGRAPHER

Good.

Looks through the viewfinder, sees that lens cap is still on camera, removes it.

Much better.

ASSISTANT

What we're going to be doing in this one is re-enacting, or re-creating—celebrating, too, really—a little-known photograph by an unknown photographer, depicting—well, you'll see. The title—though it's hard to make out the writing on the back—the title is "The Bully Composition." It was taken in 1898 in Cuba during the Spanish-American War. "The Splendid Little War." I'll pass this around, and, when you look at it, you can see how strangely the people

She looks at it for the first time and realizes she has the wrong photo. This is treated as only a minor inconvenience.

—and, oops, wrong one. Sorry. I have it here. Hang on one sec.

She begins looking through the papers in her folder, just as she is saying "…, wrong one."

Sorry.

She continues looking.

PHOTOGRAPHER

We'll wait.

Brief pause. He looks through the viewfinder.

"People in a Building, Seated, Breathing." That's what I'd title this. Or "Number Nineteen."

He looks again. Referring to people in seats the lens might not be able to include:

I don't know if we'll get everyone.

Brief pause.

We're all here in spirit.

During the above, ASSISTANT has begun looking in another folder.

PHOTOGRAPHER

He takes a quick look at the incorrect photograph that ASSISTANT was about to pass around. To ASSISTANT.

Maybe I could do my…

ASSISTANT, as she continues to look for the photograph, nods a quick "yes."

To audience:

So, I do a little thing, sort of a—I don't know, you'll see. It seems to be helpful, picture-taking-wise. It helps people get into a kind of—well, I hope it does, anyway—but just, the right place. It's probably weird, but, maybe it'll be good. So…

PHOTOGRAPHER begins a concerted effort at going into some kind of a trance. Pause.

Private…

Very long pause. ASSISTANT looks, occasionally and very discretely, for the photo. PHOTOGRAPHER doesn't go into a trance.

Sorry. Usually I can do it.

ASSISTANT

And, I don't think we have our photo. We're all right. Um, maybe it'd be good if we could…sorry, one second.

She whispers something to PHOTOGRAPHER. Very short exchange, between them, as they decide to move on.

To audience:

Okay. We're fine.

Very quick last peek into the folder.

We can live without it.

With little lingering anxiety, she moves gently and respectfully into the details of the photograph.

What you would see, if you could see it, is a group of American troops sitting on the ground and on boxes, staring at the camera. We are on San Juan Hill, in the Spanish-American War, July 1st. It was the single worst day of fighting, they say, the bloodiest. "The Bully Composition." Photographer unknown. The people in it have this sort of historic look in their eyes.

PHOTOGRAPHER

Almost like they were born to be in a photograph. Except, they don't really have any expressions. They're just regular people, staring straight ahead. As they—I don't know—as they try to gather the strength their post-photograph lives are going to ask of them.

ASSISTANT

I think they have expressions. People always have expressions. You just have to look.

Brief pause.

What else? It's black-and-white, of course. They're right there. The people. One of them looks like he wants to cry but doesn't know what crying is. Or like it's a burden for him to have a face.

Brief pause.

There's some discrepancy about the time of day.

PHOTOGRAPHER

Somewhat dismissively.

But it's fairly clear.

ASSISTANT

Well, but there are questions.

PHOTOGRAPHER

Conceding the point, somewhat.

Yes, there are questions. You can't tell from the sky if it's morning or evening. It can look like both.

ASSISTANT

Of course, the sky. But it's not just the sky. It's the meaning of the sky. The meaning of morning or evening. Were they afraid of dying, or, happy to be alive? Did they just do something awful, or were they about to do something brave? One has his legs crossed. He's holding an apple. It's such a simple picture. You'd think we'd be able to tell.

PHOTOGRAPHER

Well, the resolution isn't great. The sky looks almost like it's done in watercolor. And the flag in the background is all blurry. And, I think—I forget—I think it's torn.

ASSISTANT

A little frayed, at the end. But, yes, blurry.

PHOTOGRAPHER

The rest is very still, sharp, the people. They had to sit like that for a while, because of the old cameras. Imagine. Nobody moving. It's very quiet. Storm clouds and maybe something else are gathering. A mosquito—and this was in the days of yellow fever and malaria—a mosquito lands on your cheek and just sits there. All quiet. You wait for the click. This was the moment.

ASSISTANT

Yes, but, possibly not—which is the interesting thing. That there can be such precision regarding the actual moment, but, so much confusion regarding the context. Or, regarding the two moments on either side.

PHOTOGRAPHER

I think it's morning.

ASSISTANT

It may be, but, I guess… I don't know. If you could see it, really look into the picture of these people's eyes—I wish I had it—I think you'd see a bigger mystery other than just what time it was. Wouldn't you? Had they just come through it all? All the shattered bones and real blood and bleeding horses and noise. Or was it still just farm boys' quiet dreams of glory, something later, something fine and right, that they were about to do? Which version were they? And what's either one supposed to look like? You'd see it, I think. The confusion, the whole trouble. It'd be there in their faces, somehow, whenever it was. Imagine that: a day, a serious day, or a night, in someone else's life. Cuts and scratches, actual dirty socks; serious doubts and homesickness. Someone else's. A splinter, an unheld hand. A war. Feel *that.* Look at a picture and feel *that.*

Brief pause.

We should try and learn to look at each other harder.

Brief pause.

If we did, well, then, maybe, then, we'd all… I don't know.

PHOTOGRAPHER

Maybe.

Pause. Gently:

Why don't we try to take this.

ASSISTANT

Take what?

PHOTOGRAPHER

This.

ASSISTANT

But, this *what*? That's what I'm trying to say.

PHOTOGRAPHER

This photograph. Is what I'm trying to say.

ASSISTANT is standing somewhere in the camera's frame. Motioning her to the side.

Could you…

She moves.

And, could you move that light down?

ASSISTANT

It's easy to feel sorry for people in a photograph, to think you understand.

Adjusting the angle of a light.

It's easy to look at a picture, wince, keep looking, and say you can't look anymore.

Referring to the light.

Like that?

PHOTOGRAPHER

PHOTOGRAPHER stares into the light, a little distracted.

Yes.

Pause.

Yeah. Good.

Referring to the extra light:

We might not even need this. It's always a compromise, with light, as to whether you…

He continues to stare mainly into the light, throughout. Perhaps speaks in a heightened sort of monotone.

Private Edward Thomas; Sterling, Indiana. We're halfway up a hill that goes down the other side. Under sickening violent fire. Such insane rage over there. And over here. Mullen lost his eye and he's crying out of the other one. Foley's holding his insides. His intestines look like animals. Somebody lost a hand and it's lying in the dirt in the sun like a drawing. They told us not to shoot or move or make noise. So we're not. Americans hiding on the side of a hill, frozen still, waiting for orders. Forward or back, I don't care, but, somewhere, soon, please. It's like being in someone else's nightmare. War is not hell, it's not organized enough to be. Then you come home, if you come home, and get your picture in the paper, mangled in body or spirit. One way or the other, mother, the ghost of your boy is coming home. But not now. Still have some time and life to waste, now. I wonder if the hand is Spanish or American. No such thing as locals here. Just us and other foreigners. Poor people from around the world, shooting each other and wishing we were home. I have to pee so badly. I wonder if you will remember me or think of me, ever. A hungry nobody lying on the ground, watching ants crawling over his leg, trying not to shake, and dying for a single moment of, a single moment of, just a single second where—

Pause. He gently comes out of his trance.

Okay.

Brief pause.

All right. Good. I think that should…we're good.

ASSISTANT

With gentle concern:

Okay? Is everything all—

PHOTOGRAPHER

Interrupting.

We're good.

ASSISTANT

So…okay. I guess we're… I guess we're ready.

The following series of lines are all spoken to the audience, most of them very much as if they are gentle "directions" one might give an actor or model whose photo is being taken. Throughout, PHOTOGRAPHER will be looking through the viewfinder, making adjustments, and surveying the audience.

"Bully Composition." Here we go. There you are.

PHOTOGRAPHER

Looking through viewfinder.

There you are.

ASSISTANT

Is it morning or evening?

PHOTOGRAPHER

It's morning.

ASSISTANT

It might be evening.

PHOTOGRAPHER

Making a small adjustment to the camera. Returning to viewfinder.

You're just sitting there. All is quiet.

ASSISTANT

Or is it. Even The Hundred Years' War had a middle. A little quiet moment in the middle that somehow determined the end.

She holds for a moment, to allow for a "quiet little moment."

Like that.

PHOTOGRAPHER

Smoke starts to come out onto the stage. Looking through the viewfinder.

Good. Nice.

Noticing smoke.

I don't know what the smoke is. I think it's for something else. Don't pay any attention. I'm sure it's fine. Just be you.

ASSISTANT

On the threshold of death.

PHOTOGRAPHER

Just act natural.

ASSISTANT

You're sitting on a wooden box. There's a war going on. A real war. The blurry flag gently waves. Maybe you're about to be shot in the throat.

Quietly, plainly:

Bang.

Brief pause.

Splendid.

PHOTOGRAPHER

Good.

Looking through viewfinder.

I think this is good.

He looks again.

It might even be better.

ASSISTANT

It's really… We don't need the other photo. This is it, now. God, if you could see yourselves. So solemn. So divided. What are *you* in the middle of? How do *you* want to be remembered? What are we to see in your eyes?

PHOTOGRAPHER

Just try to sit up nice and straight.

To someone in the audience wearing glasses.

Maybe you could take your glasses off. Or, no, they're good.

To ASSISTANT:

Keep going.

ASSISTANT

Are you afraid of dying or happy to be alive? The fighting, the horror, the glory, our country—is it over or has it not even started? Show us the national dilemma, in your faces. It's beautiful. Your anxieties, your agonies. They're so photogenic.

PHOTOGRAPHER

Thanks everyone. Almost there.

ASSISTANT

A little more. Nice and gentle. Breathe. Now, feel more things. Think bigger things. This is going to be you, someday. Gorgeous. Wonderful. Be historical.

PHOTOGRAPHER

Good.

To a particular person in the audience, in response to his or her expression.

Very nice, keep that, keep that.

ASSISTANT

Show us you, trying to be better, mortally afraid.

PHOTOGRAPHER

Making adjustments to camera, exposure settings, etc.

Thank you. Last chance. Almost, almost…

ASSISTANT

Be more tragic. More forgiving. More unknowing. More mortal. Try to be more mortal. As much as you can stand.

PHOTOGRAPHER

He looks up from the viewfinder.

Yeah. Perfect.

Camera flash. Blackout.

END

OH, THE HUMANITY

Dramatis Personae

MAN

WOMAN

MAN #2

Setting

Two Chairs.

Stage.

Stage properties

A bottle of water.

Lipstick.

MAN and WOMAN are seated in two chairs, facing the audience. The chairs are arranged as if to be the front seat of a car. There are no other major props and nothing other than stage directions and the actors' gestures to indicate the existence of a car or any of its parts (such as a rearview mirror) onstage. WOMAN is putting on lipstick in the rearview mirror. MAN puts the key into the ignition, turns the key. We hear the sound effect of an engine cranking but not starting. MAN turns key again, same. MAN gets out, goes around to the front, then the back, of the car.

WOMAN

Checking her lipstick, arranging her hair.

Is it the battery?

MAN

No.

WOMAN

What is it? Are we stuck?

MAN

It's just chairs.

WOMAN

What, hon?

MAN

It's just two chairs.

WOMAN

Still arranging her hair, touching up her lipstick.

You're kidding. Just two regular chairs?

MAN

Yeah.

WOMAN

So, how do we get to the church? What time's the christening?

MAN

I thought it was a funeral.

WOMAN

Well, whichever. It was definitely a church. Now we're going to be late.

MAN

Very softly, almost to himself.

I thought it was a funeral.

WOMAN

Darling, let's not fight.

MAN

I'm not fighting. At all. Not at all.

WOMAN

No, of course you're not, I know.

Brief pause.

And even if you were: it's over, thank God. Now, what were you saying?

MAN

I thought my father died and we were going to bury him.

WOMAN

Well, that may well be. It's a busy time.

MAN

What does that mean?

WOMAN

It means, well, just think. Of all the things. All the life beyond our immediate—God, I don't even know—surroundings. Refugees pouring over borders, quintuplets being born, floods in distant countries, meteor showers, mudslides, adultery. Wheat gently blowing in a wheat field somewhere, an animal being put to sleep. Great moments in sports, boat shows, volcanoes, tornadoes, grandmothers being wheeled into nursing homes, never to see natural light again. Think of it all. God. What a busy world. Such a busy time.

She drinks from a bottle of water. Brief pause.

Medical breakthroughs, personal setbacks, embarrassing moments in literature. Millions of things. War, famine, misunderstanding. Car trouble. Simple pain in everyday settings.

Brief pause.

Boat shows. I already said that.

MAN is staring off, perhaps in mourning.

MAN

He was just mowing the lawn, yesterday.

WOMAN

She continues on.

Whales washing up on empty beaches. Home-pregnancy test kits being thrown through windows. Anniversaries, coronations, cremations, and parades. Of course, there's more, but, I'm done. Oh, and my niece being christened. And don't forget your father, his glasses sideways on his face, going to his knees in the half-cut grass, pointing at his mouth.

MAN

Brief pause.

I would like it if we could leave here. I'm going to take another look

He goes around to the back of the car.

WOMAN

Turning and resting an arm on the backs of the chairs.

Anything?

MAN

Again…

He gestures toward the chairs.

WOMAN

Ah, yes. Our predicament.

MAN

Is that what this is?

WOMAN

It's a word, okay? It describes something. So what do we do?

MAN #2

Enters. Stands quietly to the side. MAN and WOMAN notice him, but are not overly concerned with his arrival or his presence.

MAN

Lost in thought. Sadly.

My father. To his knees, like that? His glasses sideways on his face? Do you think?

WOMAN

Maybe.

MAN

And your niece?

WOMAN

Smiling, crying, reaching for something. Saliva bubbling out of her mouth. Or that's your dad. It's quite a world.

MAN

And here we are, missing it. Late for it.

Brief pause.

You know, I'm really trying. I am. To be—I don't know—to be something, to be truthful somehow, sitting here in my chair, with you, and that other chair. I'm starting to–. This is so–. I'm going to miss him. I'm really trying here. Here, in our little–.

Brief pause.

The eagle does not try. The mouse does not try. But is the eagle not in fact the mouse?

WOMAN

No.

MAN

But you get my point.

WOMAN

No.

MAN

No, okay. But, do you see a larger mystery?

WOMAN

Do I see a different mystery? Do I see stranger relations—between things and *not* between things, do I sense a wider deeper sense of wonder and mayhem? Do I feel a whole set of simple established facts missing, the rug disintegrating thread-by-thread, gone before it can even be pulled out from underneath us?

MAN

Yes.

WOMAN

I do. I think I do.

MAN

Because I'm starting to wonder.

WOMAN

To MAN #2:

Do you know anything about cars?

MAN #2

Oh. No. I mean, I know that they're convenient.

WOMAN

Who are you?

MAN #2

It's a little embarrassing. You're probably going to laugh. But, I'm the beauty of things, the majesty of—I don't know—the world? The Universe? Although, just to let you know, I don't possess any secret knowledge or any glimpse into anything, so, I wouldn't bother to, you know…

MAN and WOMAN return their attentions to each other.

MAN

To WOMAN.

Because, like I said, I'm starting to wonder. To wonder, and, struggle a little, here. In our world in which so much is happening, reportedly.

WOMAN

Checking her watch.

We should almost be there.

MAN

Quietly.

Where?

WOMAN

Checking her watch.

We're definitely late.

MAN

I'm trying. I am, so hard. To make the best of this. To not just start shouting. To not start hating you just because I'm afraid and I don't understand. Or start crying. I'm trying, Vanessa.

Pause. He is almost crying, though managing to cover it, to control himself.

But, these are chairs. And I don't know where… I don't know what we're supposed to do. And I want my father. I miss my dad. There's some stranger standing here. And these are chairs. And that's it. And I don't know who I am.

WOMAN

There there.

Pause.

Isn't that awful? How far can you push a person away, with just two words? "There there."

MAN

Very brief pause.

That's it?

WOMAN

What? People expect people to be so loving in these situations.

MAN

"These situations?"

WOMAN

I don't know. How am I supposed to know? You think I'm not trying, too? You, me, and two stupid chairs—and you're so surprised that I haven't made a more stable, more substantial, more loving life for myself, for us? I thought we were going to a christening. Maybe a baptism. The little baby, all in white, waiting for a name. Some incense, some soothing inscrutable Latin, a chance to see everyone. A ritual, any ritual, just something to take pictures of. A Bat Mitzvah or a Hindu Naming Ceremony, I don't care. I had one tiny wish. Let's go somewhere and see something. An innocent beginning or a gruesome end, anything. But, alas, it seems, No.

MAN

I'm trying to picture him. Whatever suit they put him in.

WOMAN

Her little hands and those big eyes, looking up, or, asleep. As they say prayers for her name or whatever they do. Her mouth a little mess of saliva.

MAN

His glasses on, nice and straight. Him all dressed up. Everyone there.

WOMAN

And the sunlight through the stained-glass windows. Everyone there. The otherworldly music.

MAN

All the skinny undertakers, outside, smoking. Him all dry, all preserved. He was mowing the lawn, yesterday. Bye, Dad.

WOMAN

Katie is a pretty name. I do love their little hands and the great big eyes. Katie, maybe. It'd be nice if they decided on "Katie."

MAN #2

From where he has been standing, MAN #2 begins speaking to the audience.

It would probably come as no surprise to you were I to suddenly move closer to you, now.

He does not move.

It would come as no surprise, I'm sure, were I to suddenly begin my speech, to bring it all home, as we all move closer and closer. All of us certain of simple things, certain in our knowledge that we are loved, that people love us, that God loves us, that God exists and loves us, that people exist and love us.

A general pause.

I can see from your faces. That that would come as no surprise. For me to do something very expected like that.

Brief pause.

Ah. Your faces. So fragile, so certain. The majesty.

Lights fade.

END

WILL ENO is a fellow of Residency Five at Signature Theatre Company in New York. His play *The Open House* premiered at Signature in 2014, and received an Obie Award, the Lucille Lortel Award for Best Play, and a Drama Desk Special Award. His play *The Realistic Joneses* premiered at Yale Repertory Theatre in 2012, and was produced on Broadway in 2014, for which he and the cast received a Drama Desk Special Award. His play *Title and Deed* premiered at Signature in 2012 and was presented at the Edinburgh Fringe Festival in 2014. Both *Title and Deed* and *The Realistic Joneses* were included in the *New York Times* Best Plays List of 2012. *Gnit*, an adaption of Ibsen's *Peer Gynt*, premiered at Actors Theatre of Louisville in 2013. *Middletown*, winner of the Horton Foote Prize, premiered at the Vineyard Theatre in New York in 2010, and was then produced at Steppenwolf Theatre Company in Chicago in 2011. *Thom Pain (based on nothing)* was a finalist for the 2005 Pulitzer Prize and has been translated into many languages. *The Flu Season* premiered at the Gate Theatre in London in 2003, and later received the Oppenheimer Award for best New York debut production by an American writer. *Tragedy: a tragedy* premiered at the Gate Theatre in 2001, and was subsequently produced by Berkeley Repertory Theatre in 2008. Mr. Eno lives in Brooklyn with his wife Maria Dizzia and their daughter Albertine.

Printed in the USA
CPSIA information can be obtained
at www.ICGtesting.com
JSHW082359140824
68134JS00020B/2174